Welcome aboard!

Join canyon

This year, you are going on an amazing handwriting journey to a world of joins and fluency.
Be sure to have your passport ready.

Handwriting Passport

Name: _____

Age: _____

Five things about me:

1 _____

2 _____

3 _____

4 _____

5 _____

Approved!

Exit harbour

Horizontal cove

City entry

Diagonal mountains

Trace then copy.

Remember to sit the letters on the baseline correctly.

q   f   e

s   a   g

q   c   o

s   d   e

Make up your own patterns using these letter shapes.

Trace then copy.

Think about where you
will start each letter.

START

n   r

m   h

k   x

r   3

Make up your own patterns using these letter shapes.

Handwriting: clockwise fluency patterns; lower-case letters revision.

Trace then copy.

Remember to keep the slope the same.

Make up your own patterns using these letter shapes.

Trace then copy.

Remember to keep
the slope the same.

Make up your own patterns using these letter shapes.

Handwriting: fluency patterns; lower-case u family letters.

Make the letters stretch and shrink.

Handwriting: forming letters correctly; keeping slope consistent. **Literary elements:** reference to characters from *Alice's Adventures in Wonderland*, by Lewis Carroll (1865).

Capital letters always sit on the baseline.

Trace then write the capitals.
Underline the capitals that use downward strokes.

A B C D

E F G H

I J K L

M N O P

Q R S T

U V W X

Y Z

Write the missing capital letters.

A ___ C D ___ ___ G H ___

___ L ___ N P ___ R S

V ___ ___ ___ Z

Handwriting: capital letters revision; capitals always sit on the baseline. **Spelling:** alphabetical order. **Literary elements:** visual reference to Aesop fable, *The Lion and the Mouse.*

Use this alphabet to spell out words when you want to be clearly understood.

Trace the NATO alphabet.

Alpha   Bravo   Charlie

Delta   Echo   Foxtrot

Golf   Hotel   India

Juliet   Kilo   Lima

Mike   November   Oscar

Papa   Quebec   Romeo

Sierra   Tango   Uniform

Victor   Whiskey   X-ray

Yankee   Zulu

Spell your name in the NATO alphabet.

Handwriting: lower-case and capital letters revision. **Spelling and vocabulary:** alphabetical order; codes; NATO alphabet.

8

Trace the capital letter and then make up your own alphabet.

A   B   C

D   E   F

G   H   I

J   K   L

M   N   O

P   Q   R

S   T   U

V   W   X

Y   Z

Spell a friend's name in your new alphabet.

Handwriting: lower-case and capital letters revision. **Spelling and vocabulary:** alphabetical order; codes.

Review: Labelling diagrams

Use these words to label the robot. Use your best capital letters.

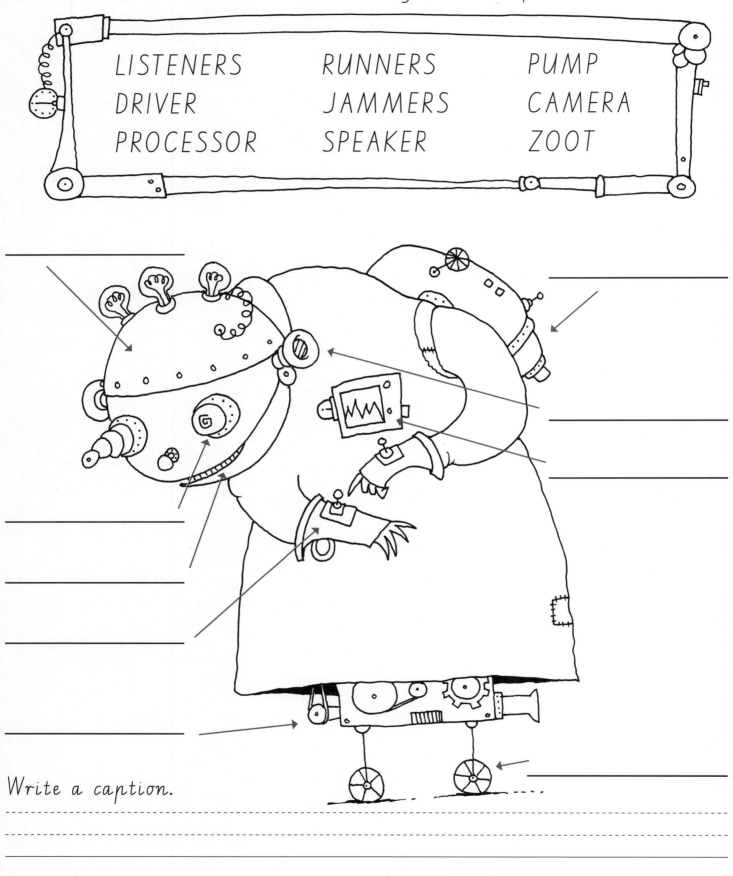

LISTENERS   RUNNERS   PUMP
DRIVER   JAMMERS   CAMERA
PROCESSOR   SPEAKER   ZOOT

Write a caption.

Handwriting: using capital letters to label diagrams. **Spelling and vocabulary:** technical vocabulary. **Literary elements:** science fiction genre.

Trace then copy.

. .   , ,   ? ?   ! !

: :   ; ;   - -   — —

' '   " "   " "

Trace then write.

"What do you call a collection

of letters?" asked the teacher.

"That's the alphabet!" shouted

the class.

That elephant can spell!

e

Handwriting: punctuation revision. **Grammar:** collective noun (class); saying verbs (asked, shouted). **Punctuation:** full stop; comma; question mark; exclamation mark; colon; semi-colon; hyphen; dash; apostrophe; speech marks. **Spelling and vocabulary:** apostrophe for contraction (that's).

11

Trace then write.

0   5

1   6

2   7

3   8

4   9

Write numerals to answer each question.

What year were you born? _____

What is your phone number? _____

What time do you get up in the morning?

_____

What time do you go to bed on a school night?

_____

What time does school start? _____

Handwriting: numerals revision. **Grammar:** questions.

Watch your letter size, letter shape and slope. Make sure your letters face the right way.

Rewrite the text correctly.

"WHat dO You CAll a grOUP

of chilDren?" asked SanJay.

"That's a sLazz!" yellEd RoSie.

"You're corrEct".

Self-assessment

My letter shapes: need to improve ☐ are good ☐ are fantastic ☐.

My letter sizes: are inconsistent ☐ are good ☐ are fantastic ☐.

My letter slope: is inconsistent ☐ is good ☐ is consistently good ☐.

Handwriting: slope; letter shape; letter size. **Grammar:** question; exclamation; saying verbs (asked, yelled); collective noun (class).
Punctuation: full stop; capital letter to start a sentence; exclamation mark; question mark; speech marks. **Spelling and vocabulary:** apostrophe for contraction (that's).

Practise quick exits from these letters.

Trace then write.

a .

d .

c .

e .

a .

d .

c .

e .

Trace then write.

ace aced add added dead

Remember! Try to keep your
writing hand relaxed.

Trace then write.

m

n

h

p

x

k

Trace then write.

man knack hack axe pen

peace happen name came

Handwriting: developing rhythm for diagonal exits from clockwise letters. **Spelling and vocabulary:** rhyme (name/came, knack/hack).

Trace then write.

i

t

l

u

Trace then write.

hill mill nil pill till

hut nut cut mutt putt

lit pit kit hit knit mitt

Handwriting: developing rhythm for diagonal exits from i and u family letters. **Spelling and vocabulary:** rhyme.

Practise horizontal exits from these letters at the top body line.

Trace then write.

v   w

f

b

o

r

Trace then write.

bone   worm

hole   rove

dog   wag

Handwriting: developing rhythm for horizontal exits.

Practise rounded entries to these letters.

m n r x z

Trace then write each letter.

m

n

r

x

z

Trace then write.

man   box

razor   oxen

maze   haze

narrow

marrow

Handwriting: rounded entries n, m, r, x and z. **Spelling and vocabulary:** rhyme (narrow/marrow).

The author Roald Dahl often made up words of his own.

Trace then write.

"Here is the repulsant

snozzcumber!" cried the BFG,

waving it about. "I squoggle it!

I mispise it! I dispunge it!"

Make up some words of your own.

_____

_____

_____

_____

Handwriting: entries and exits. **Grammar:** statement; exclamation; adjective (repulsant); speaking verb (cried); action verb (waving); feeling verbs (squoggle, mispise, dispunge); noun (snozzcumber); noun-pronoun reference chain (snozzcumber/it); acronym (BFG).
Punctuation: full stop; capital letter to start a sentence; exclamation mark; comma; speech marks. **Spelling and vocabulary:** negative prefixes mis- (in mispise for despise), dis- (in dispunge meaning to expunge or erase). **Literary elements:** quote from *The BFG*, by Roald Dahl (1982); neologism (snozzcumber); portmanteau word (repulsant = repulsive and unpleasant).

Remember the 3 p's: posture, pencil hold, paper position.

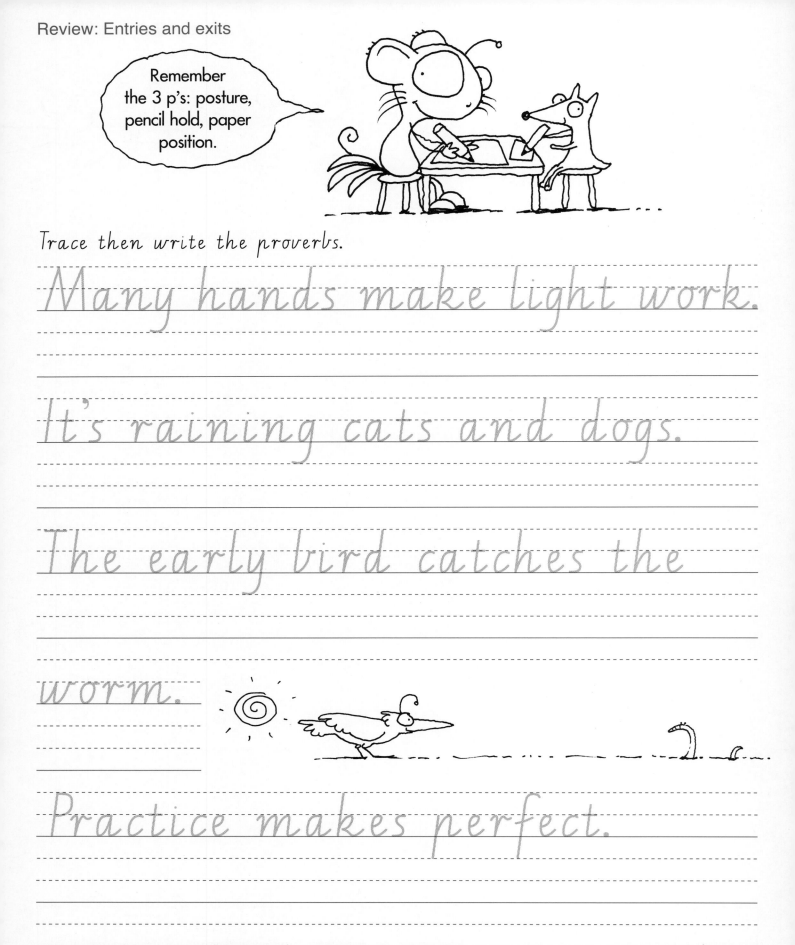

Trace then write the proverbs.

Many hands make light work.

It's raining cats and dogs.

The early bird catches the

worm.

Practice makes perfect.

Handwriting: entries and exits. **Grammar:** adjectives (light, early); common nouns (hands, work, cats, dogs, bird, worm, practice). **Punctuation:** full stop; capital letter to start a sentence. **Spelling and vocabulary:** apostrophe for contraction (it's). **Literary elements:** proverbs; idiom.

Trace then write the spoonerisms.

picking your nose -

nicking your pose

jelly beans - belly jeans

jumpy puppy - pumpy juppy

trail snacks - snail tracks

eye ball - bye all

TRAIL SNACKS

Handwriting: entries and exits. **Spelling and vocabulary**: rhyme. **Literary elements**: spoonerisms.

Trace then write.

In the sea, once

upon a time . . . there was a

Whale, and he ate fishes.

He ate the starfish and the

garfish . . . and the really

truly twirly-whirly eel.

Handwriting: entries and exits. **Punctuation:** ellipsis to indicate words have been left out (. . .). **Spelling and vocabulary:** rhyme (twirly-whirly). **Literary elements:** quote from *Just So Stories*, 'How the Whale Got His Throat', by Rudyard Kipling (1902); common story beginning phrase 'once upon a time'.

Trace then write.

a c d e h i k l m

Diagonal joins **follow** these letters.

n p q s t u x

Trace then write.

b f o r v w

Horizontal joins **follow** these letters.

No joins follow these letters.

Trace then write.

g j y z

Trace then write.

a c d g q

To **join to** these letters, lift your pencil and drop in the letter.

Handwriting: letter groups with common exits for joins; letters that don't join yet; letters that require touch joins with a pencil lift.

23

A diagonal join links to the next letter at the top of the next letter's body.

an ←baseline

Look for the capital A inside the join.

u → u → u → up

Make an exit . . .   then keep going up . . .   until you get to the start of the next letter.

Trace then write the letter pairs. Use diagonal joins.

up   ur   um   un   ui   uy

ar   ai   aj   am   an   au

av   aw   ap   di   dr   du

Handwriting: diagonal joins to body letters and to body and tail letters (descenders). **Spelling:** common letter pairs.

Remember to look for the capital A inside each join.

Trace then write the letter pairs.

mi mu mm my mp mn an

ni nn nu ny kr ki kn

ku hy hi hu im in ly

ir ly li lu lp lm ti

ty tw tu tr ei em en

er ew ny ep ki kn lp

Handwriting: diagonal joins to body letters and to body and tail letters (descenders). **Spelling:** common letter pairs.

Diagonal joins

Trace then write the letter pairs.

ci cy cu ci cy cu ci cy cu

py pi pu pp pi pu pp

xy xi xi xy xi xi

ty ti tu ty ti tu

To join diagonally to o, go to the top of the o and retrace back.

co po to ao do ho

ko lo mo no uo io ko lo

My diagonal joins are smooth: sometimes ☐ often ☐ always ☐.

Handwriting: diagonal joins to body and to body and tail letters (descenders); diagonal joins to o. **Spelling:** common letter pairs.

To connect a diagonal join to a tall head and body letter, continue the exit all the way up to the top.

u → *u* → *u* → *u* *u* *ut*

Make an   keep going up . . . to the very top . . . then retrace to make
exit . . .   the next letter.

Trace then write the letter pairs. Use diagonal joins.

ik   il   it   ib   ub   ul   ut

uk   mb   ml   nb   nh   nt

nk   nl   ab   ah   at   ak   al

cl   ch   ck   ct   cl   el   et

Handwriting: diagonal joins to head and body letters (ascenders). **Spelling:** common letter pairs.

Diagonal joins

Le → Le

unjoined e   joined e

To make a diagonal join to e, change the shape of the e slightly.

Trace then write.

ie   ae   ue   ce   xe   me

le   de   he   ke   pe   ee

keen   mean   dean   scene

To make a diagonal join to x, you need to swing around smoothly.

a → as → ax²

Make a diagonal exit . . .   and swing around smoothly to x.   Lift your pencil and form the second stroke of x.

Trace then write.

ax   ax   ix   ix   ex   ex

ax   ax   ix   ix   ex   ex

tax   six   text   mix   max

Handwriting: diagonal joins to e and x. **Spelling and vocabulary:** common letter pairs; rhyme.

28

To join
to f, use
a loop.

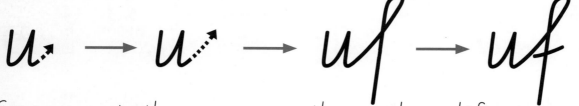

Go up . . .   to the   then make   Lift your pencil
               top body line . . .   a loop.   and add the crossbar.

Trace then write.

f f f

lf   *af*

if   *uf*

gulf leaf deaf gift sift lift

life wife strife thief chief

Write words of your own with f.

Handwriting: diagonal joins to f. **Spelling and vocabulary:** rhyme (gift/sift, life/wife).

Use a diagonal join to link q to u.

q → q → q → qu

Continue the exit all the way up to the top body line.

Trace then write.

q q q q

qu qu qu qu

quest   quiver   quill   queen

"Please quit making a racket

with that racquet!" he quipped.

Twang

Handwriting: diagonal joins q to u. **Punctuation:** speech marks; exclamation mark. **Spelling and vocabulary:** u always follows q; homophones.

To make a faster diagonal join to s, change the shape of the s.

top of s is much shorter

a → *a* → *as*

Make a diagonal exit . . .   keep going to make a short top on the s . . .   then quickly retrace and go around.

Trace then write.

es   is   us   as   es   is   us   as

ds   hs   ks   ls   ts   ms   ns   ps

games names blames flames

cans fans pans plans hands

Self-assessment   When I write, my hand and arm are relaxed and comfortable: rarely ☐ mostly ☐ always ☐ .

Handwriting: diagonal joins to s. **Spelling and vocabulary:** rhyme.

Diagonal joins

To make a diagonal join from s, you need to retrace.

retrace **sk**   **ask**
                    retrace

Retrace the bottom of the s.
Then go up to make a diagonal join.

Trace then write.

si su si su si su sink sunk

sp st sp st sp st spill slip

so so so soap soak

st st st stink stunk

Self-assessment

I retraced neatly: sometimes ☐ often ☐ always ☐ .

Handwriting: diagonal joins from s. **Spelling and vocabulary:** rhyme (stink/sink).

Trace then write to practise joins to and from s.

ish ish ish wish fish dish

ist ist ist list fist mist

Trace then write. Use diagonal joins where you need to.

knight night

knit nit

cent sent scent

wait weight

sail sale

meat meet

Did you see the nit knit?

Handwriting: diagonal joins to and from s, revision. **Punctuation:** question mark. **Spelling and vocabulary**: rhyme (list/ mist, wish/dish); common letter pairs (gh, kn, ee, ea); homophones.

Make sure your joins are smooth and you retrace neatly.

Trace then write.

loan lone

main mane

rain pane

pair pear

paw pour

rain rein

raw roar

hear here

Will you pour with that paw?

Handwriting: diagonal joins revision. **Punctuation:** question mark. **Spelling and vocabulary:** homophones.

Trace then write.

Practise more diagonal joins.

cue queue

days daze

blew blue

quay key

knew new

tail tale

eight ate

maize maze

Write a sentence of your own using one or more of the word pairs.

Self-assessment

My diagonal joins are smooth: sometimes ☐ often ☐ always ☐.

I retraced neatly: sometimes ☐ often ☐ always ☐.

Handwriting: diagonal joins revision. **Spelling and vocabulary:** homophones.

To join from a letter that finishes near the top body line (b, f, o, r, v and w) you need a horizontal join.

by or ry

A horizontal join is a line with a little wave.

Trace then write.

vi　　vu　　wi　　wu

oi　　om　　ou　　on

op　　or　　ov　　ox

oz　　rm　　ri　　ru

rr　　ry　　rp　　by

bu　　bi　　wn　　wy

toy　　top　　oil　　burp

Handwriting: horizontal joins from letters that finish near the top body line (b, f, o, r, v and w). **Spelling:** digraphs 'oy' (toy), 'oi' (oil), 'ur' (burp).

To make a horizontal join to b, h, k, l or t, you need to retrace.

w → w ⌐ → w⌐l → wh

From the exit ... go up ... then retrace down.

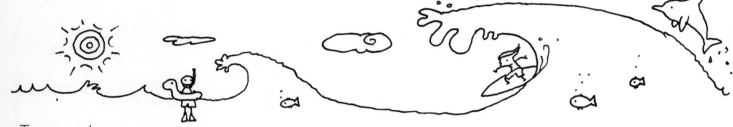

Trace then write.

wh who what where which

rt girl curl hurl whirl twirl

rk work rk lurk rt shirt

Self-assessment

My retracing is smooth and neat: rarely ☐ mostly ☐ always ☐.

Handwriting: horizontal joins to head and body letters (ascenders) b, h, k, l, t. **Grammar:** question words/pronouns (who, what, where, which).
Spelling and vocabulary: digraph 'wh' (who, what, where, which); rhyme (girl, curl, hurl, whirl, twirl).

Horizontal joins

To make a horizontal join to o, continue the exit stroke to the starting point of o then retrace a little.

Trace then write.

oo   ro   bo   vo   wo   oo

hoot room boil worm

oh ooh Pooh Pharaoh

Pooh's Hunny

pool cool drool hoot

book hook cook look took

Look how Pooh spells honey.

Handwriting: horizontal joins to o. **Grammar:** interjections (oh, ooh); proper nouns (Pharaoh, Pooh). **Spelling and vocabulary:** rhyme (book/took, cool/pool); digraph 'oo'. **Literary elements:** reference to character (Winnie-the-Pooh) from *When We Were Very Young*, by AA Milne (1924).

38

To make a horizontal join to s, retrace the top of the s.

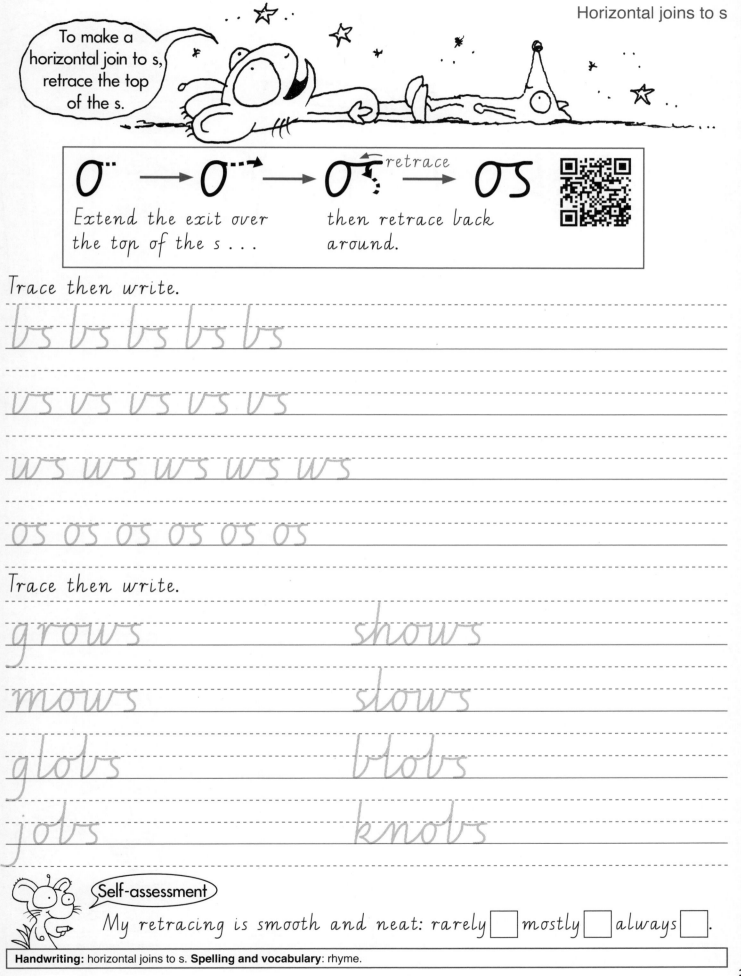

Extend the exit over the top of the s . . .

then retrace back around.

retrace

Trace then write.

bs bs bs bs bs

vs vs vs vs vs

ws ws ws ws ws

os os os os os os

Trace then write.

grows

shows

mows

slows

globs

blobs

jobs

knobs

Self-assessment

My retracing is smooth and neat: rarely ☐ mostly ☐ always ☐ .

Handwriting: horizontal joins to s. **Spelling and vocabulary:** rhyme.

To join from f, use the crossbar.

horizontal join at crossbar

fr fs fe fi

Trace then write

fe fe

fi fi

fo fo

fu fu

fr fr

fs fs

fe fi fo fum

Look out tummy! Here I come.

Handwriting: horizontal joins from f, joining f along the crossbar. **Spelling and vocabulary:** rhyme (fum/come). **Literary elements:** reference to folk tale, *Jack and the Beanstalk*.

To make a horizontal join to f, use a loop.

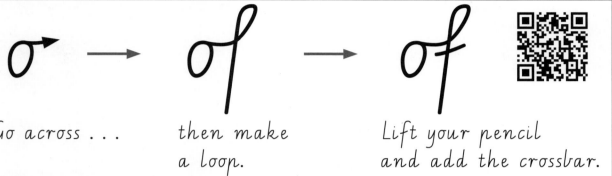

Go across . . .

then make a loop.

Lift your pencil and add the crossbar.

Trace then write.

wf awful dwarf of soft hoof

rf powerful wonderful

To make a double f, swing the first crossbar up to start the second loop.

off offer fluffy puffy stuffy

Handwriting: horizontal joins to f. **Spelling and vocabulary**: suffix (ful); rhyme (fluffy/puffy/stuffy).

be be dip

To join e, dip down.

To make a horizontal join to e, you need to dip down.

Trace then write.

vet bet wet poet rest

a tribe of goats

a shiver of sharks

a drey of squirrels

Trace.

I have a very large, hot dog.

I have a very large hot dog.

Handwriting: horizontal joins to e. **Grammar:** collective nouns. **Punctuation:** comma.

Practise horizontal joins.

Trace then write these words for sounds. Draw a star under the head and body letters where you needed to retrace.

whiz whirr growl wham

bawl hoot snarl snort sniffle

whack whoosh whoop

woof chortle burp

Hoot

Snort

Write some onomatopoeia words of your own. Tick any horizontal joins where you needed to retrace.

Handwriting: horizontal joins revision. **Spelling and vocabulary:** digraphs 'oo' (whoosh, woof, hoot, whoop), 'aw' (bawl), 'or' (snort, chortle), 'ar' (snarl). **Literary elements:** onomatopoeia.

Remember to make your letters a consistent size.

Trace then write.

ow tow show snow blow

ow window shadow ri wriggle

ri ripe script wrist ru run

ru rust runny rp burp slurp

rr purr ry hurry blurry

Handwriting: horizontal joins revision. **Spelling and vocabulary:** digraphs 'ur' (burp, slurp), 'ow' (snow), double 'rr' (blurry, purr, hurry), silent w (wriggle, wrist).

Practise horizontal joins.

Trace then write.

oi toil om stomp ou should

on only op open oy joy boy

or short vi vine or story

ow town oz dozen ob slob

ot dotty ok poke of toffee scoff

Look at the double crossbar for tt on the word dotty.

Handwriting: horizontal joins revision. **Spelling and vocabulary:** digraphs 'ou' (should), 'oi' (toil), 'or' (short, story).

Practise more horizontal joins!

Trace then write the similes.

as hungry as a wolf

as wary as a fox

as loyal as a dog

surfs like a clown

drools like a hungry monster

as cold as ice

Handwriting: horizontal joins revision. **Literary elements:** similes using 'like' or 'as'; reference to folk tale, *Little Red Riding Hood*

46

Letters with a tail pointing to the left do not join to the next letter.

g j y 3

Follow the dotted lines. These letters end with a tail pointing left. They do **not** join to the next letter.

Trace each letter pair. Remember, the letters don't join.
Write a word for each letter pair. Some have been done for you.

gl glove   go   ge

gy gypsy   gr   gi

ga   je jelly   ju

ja   ji   jo

ju   yp type   ye

ya   yo yolk   yu

yi   3a   3e zebra

3y lazy   3o   3u

Handwriting: letters that don't join yet. Spelling: common letter pairs.

Touch joins

The anticlockwise letters that start at one o'clock (a, c, d, g and q) are dropped into place. To join to them, lift your pencil.

lift pencil here

u → u → u → u a

Make an exit . . .   keep going up . . .   then lift your pencil and drop in the letter.

Trace then write. Remember to make a long exit stroke, lift your pencil and drop in the second letter.

ua   ud   ug   uc

ug   ug   iq   ka

ad   ic   ha   la

Lifting your pencil means your hand can take a break and you won't have to retrace.

Trace then write. Put a tick above the touch joins.

Fern loved Wilbur

more than anything.

Handwriting: touch joins to anticlockwise letters that start at one o'clock (a, c, d, g, and q) after letters with exits. (Touch joins at ed, ha and ng in quote.) **Literary elements:** quote from *Charlotte's Web*, by EB White (1952).

48

lift pencil here

wa

After a horizontal exit from b, f, o, r, v or w, go across a little and drop in the letter.

Trace then write.

ba   fa   oa   ra   wa

oc   rc   va   og   rg

rd   od   wd   fa   ba

band   grand   trace   face

strip

The brave dog flew grandly

over the crowd.

Handwriting: touch joins to anticlockwise letters that start at one o'clock (a, c, d, g and q). **Spelling and vocabulary:** rhyme (trace, face); common letter pairs.

Drop a letter (a, c, d, g or q) in to each word. Then write the word.

m ny   bo t

du k   bla k

gru ge   l ter

cr ck   fud e

slud e   foo

li uid   bou uet

a ua   t ke

m ke   fro

mu dy   l ke

b nd   lar e

I feel confident about touch joins:
sometimes ☐ often ☐ always ☐.

Handwriting: touch joins to anticlockwise letters that start at one o'clock (a, c, d, g and q). **Spelling:** blend '-dge' (fudge, sludge).

Make sure your dropped in letter touches the exit of the letter in front of it.

Trace then write five words for each letter pair. The first one has been done for you.

ud mud thud cloud proud loud

da

ic

wa

oa

ld

ac

ta

rd

ug

ba

Handwriting: touch joins to anticlockwise letters that start at one o'clock (a, c, d, g and q). **Spelling:** common letter pairs.

Take special care
with the touch joins.

Trace then write.

Pinocchio was made of wood.

Pippi had red hair.

Mowgli lived in the jungle.

Find some other book character names that use touch joins. Write them here in your best writing.

Self-assessment I enjoy writing with joined letters:
sometimes ☐ usually ☐ always ☐ .

Handwriting: touch joins revision. **Grammar**: proper nouns (Pippi, Mowgli, Pinocchio). **Punctuation**: capital letters for proper nouns and to start sentences; full stops at the end of sentences. **Literary elements**: references to characters from *Pippi Longstocking*, by Astrid Lindgren (1945), *The Jungle Book*, by Rudyard Kipling (1894), and *The Adventures of Pinocchio*, by Carlo Collodi (1883).

Trace then write.

"Why did you call him Tortoise,

if he wasn't one?" Alice asked.

"We called him Tortoise

because he taught us," said the

Mock Turtle angrily.

Handwriting: practising all joins. **Grammar:** question; question word (why); proper nouns (Tortoise, Mock Turtle); pronouns (you, him, he, we, us); conjunction (because). **Punctuation:** speech marks; question mark; comma; full stop; capital letter for proper nouns and to start a sentence. **Spelling and vocabulary:** apostrophe for contraction (wasn't); digraphs 'au' (because, taught), 'or' (tortoise). **Literary elements:** pun/word play (tortoise/taught us); quote from *Alice's Adventures in Wonderland*, by Lewis Carroll (1865).

Practise all your joins with this rhyming slang.

Ruff wuff

Woof

Trace then write. Link each underlined noun group with its meaning in the box.

Look out for a Noah's Ark.

Have a butcher's hook.

What's the John Dory?

Let's hit the frog and toad.

a look   the road

the story   a shark

Handwriting: practising all joins. **Grammar:** noun groups; proper nouns (Noah's Ark, John Dory); question; possessive apostrophes (Noah's, butcher's, dog's). **Punctuation:** question mark. **Literary elements:** rhyming slang.

This is a quote from a story called *The Tale of Peter Rabbit*.

Trace then write.

Don't go into Mr McGregor's

garden: your Father had

an accident there; he was

put in a pie by Mrs McGregor.

Write a safety warning of your own. It can be a warning for a friend, family member, or story character. It can be sensible or silly.

Handwriting: practising all joins. **Grammar:** warnings (Don't); commands start with a verb or verb group (Do not go); possessive apostrophe (Mr McGregor's); proper nouns (McGregor). **Punctuation:** colon; semicolon; contraction (Don't). **Literary elements**: play on words and understatement (accident/put in a pie); quote from *The Tale of Peter Rabbit*, Beatrix Potter (1902).

This quote is from a story called *The Road to Oz*. Polychrome is the Rainbow's daughter.

Trace then write.

"Haven't you any dewdrops, or

mist-cakes, or cloudbuns?"

asked Polychrome, longingly.

"'Course not," replied Dorothy.

Dewdrops, mist-cakes and cloudbuns are food that Polychrome likes to eat.
Make up some food words of your own that you think sound delicious.

Trace the nonsense poem.

JABBERWOCKY, Lewis Carroll

'Twas brillig,

and the slithy toves

Did gyre and gimble

in the wabe:

All mimsy were the borogoves,

And the mome raths outgrabe.

Here are some more nonsense words. Write a meaning for each one.
Then complete the table with some more nonsense words of your own.

NONSENSE WORDS	PART OF SPEECH	MEANING
snismy	adjective	
groot	verb	
	noun	

Handwriting: practising all joins. **Grammar:** parts of speech. **Punctuation:** apostrophe; comma; colon. **Spelling and vocabulary:** nonsense words; portmanteau words (slithy = lithe and slimy, mimsy = miserable and flimsy). **Literary elements:** poetry (ballad); quote from 'Jabberwocky' from *Through the Looking Glass*, by Lewis Carroll (1872).

Consolidation

Write a list of 10 things you'd like to do when you are older. Your ideas can be crazy or serious. It's up to you . . . just as long as you write them in your best joined handwriting. Don't forget to number your list 1 to 10.

Ten things to do challenge

A comma can make a big difference to meaning.

Copy the sentence that is a caption for the picture.

Kenji walked on, his head held high.

Kenji walked on his head, held high.

Trace then write. Then illustrate each sentence.

Let's eat Dad.

Let's eat, Dad.

Consolidation

Dr Doolittle is a story character who could talk to animals. This is a quote from him.

HEAD AND SHOULDERS OF A HORSE

FISH TAIL

SCIENTIFIC NAME: HIPPOCAMPUS PIPPITOPITUS

Copy it in your best joined handwriting.

"Oh that," said the Doctor, turning around - "that's a Wiff-Waff. Its full name is hippocampus pippitopitus."

Make up your own creature and give it a scientific sounding name. Draw a picture of it. Label its features.

Remember to use capital letters for labels.

Handwriting: practising all joins; using capital letters to label diagrams. **Grammar:** pronouns (that, that's, its). **Punctuation:** speech marks; comma. **Spelling and vocabulary:** made-up words. **Literary elements:** quote from *The Voyages of Doctor Doolittle*, by Hugo Lofting (1922).

Add as many labels as you can think of to the map. Use capital letters.

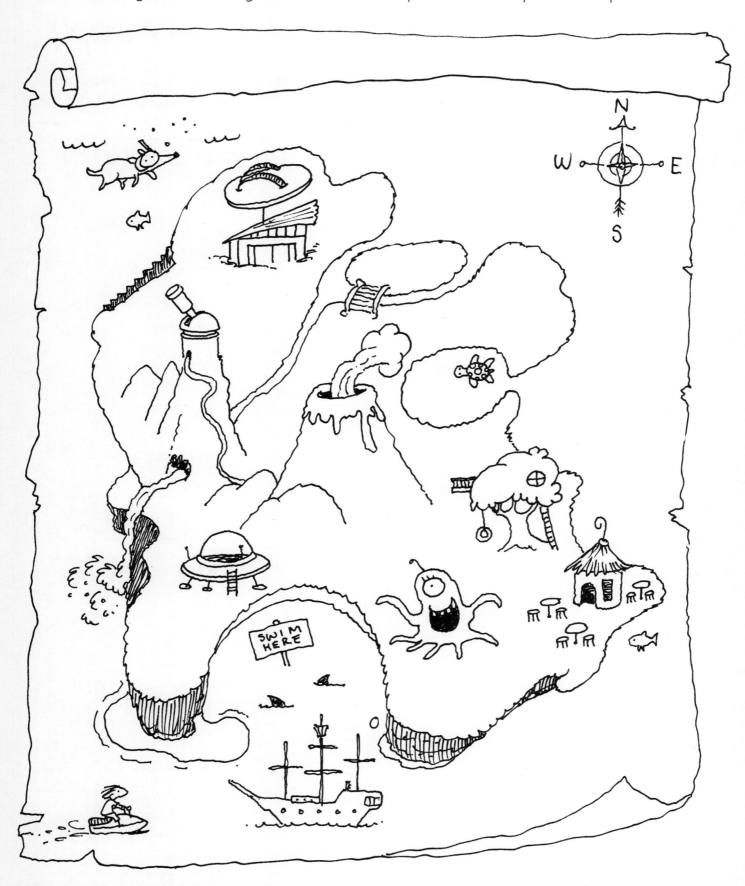

SWIM HERE

Handwriting: using capital letters to label maps and diagrams. **Literary elements:** fantasy.

61

All was a-shake and a-shiver — glints and gleams and sparkles, rustle and swirl, chatter and bubble.

Assessment 1   Date _____

Rewrite the text above using your best handwriting.

Assessment 2   Date _____

Rewrite the text above using your best handwriting.

Grammar: adjectives; common nouns; action verbs; saying verbs. **Literary elements:** quote from *The Wind in Willows*, by Kenneth Grahame (1908).

All was a-shake and a-shiver — glints and gleams and sparkles, rustle and swirl, chatter and bubble.

Assessment 3
Date _____

Rewrite the text above using your best handwriting.

Assessment 4
Date _____

Rewrite the text above using your best handwriting.

Grammar: adjectives; common nouns; action verbs; saying verbs. **Literary elements:** quote from *The Wind in Willows*, by Kenneth Grahame (1908).

Read each of the criteria listed below. When you think you have achieved each one, write the date and sign off.

My letters are the right shape. ☐ _____

My letters are a consistent size. ☐ _____

My letters are a consistent height. ☐ _____

My letters sit on the base line correctly. ☐ _____

My letter tails hang down correctly. ☐ _____

My letters are the same slope. ☐ _____

The space between my letters is regular. ☐ _____

The space between my words is regular. ☐ _____

My joins are smooth. ☐ _____

I can do all the joins. ☐ _____

My writing flows. ☐ _____

I can write quite quickly when I need to. ☐ _____

Others can easily read my joined handwriting. ☐ _____

Have you signed off on each of the criteria for fluent and legible handwriting? You've successfully completed your handwriting journey.

Congratulations!